How to be a Leader

Keys to Effective Leadership

Introduction

I want to thank you and congratulate you for buying the book, *"How to be a Leader: Keys to Effective Leadership."*

There are many definitions and theories that attempt to define leadership. Many of these are many words put together to explain the same thing. To put it in the simplest of terms, a leader is someone who guides others to accomplish a specified task. Different people use different leadership styles. This is either naturally or by training. This brings us to another issue people always ask. Are leaders born or do we learn to be leaders? I would say both are correct. Some people are naturally endowed with the abilities to lead others while other people make an effort to learn how to be effective leaders. No matter the case, we can always improve our leadership abilities by consciously making an effort to be better. Leadership is dynamic and different situations and different people will require different skills to lead them. For instance the leadership style used in a military setting is very different to the one used in a corporate setting.

In this book, we shall look at how you can refine your skills and become an effective leader.

Disclaimer

The information herein is geared towards giving definite and dependable data concerning the theme and issue covered. The distribution is sold with the understanding that the distributor, writer or publisher is not qualified or otherwise to give medical, legal or financial advice. In the event that guidance is needed, a legitimate or proficient person in the profession ought to be sought.

It is unlawful to repeat, copy, or retransmit any piece of this document by either electronic means or in printed configuration. Redistribution of this production in any capacity is not permitted unless the redistributor has explicit consent from the author or publisher. All rights held.

The information herein is understood to be truthful. In that any risk, regarding use or misuse, of any approaches, techniques, or direction contained inside is the lone and utter responsibility of the reader. By no means will any legitimate or illegitimate obligation or fault be held against the distributor, publisher, author or other, for any reparation, harms, or money related misfortune because of the data herein, either straightforward or by implication.

Particular creators possess all copyrights not held by the distributor.

The data thus is offered for information purposes only. The presentation of the data is without contract or any kind of insurance certification.

The trademarks that are utilized are without any consent or support by the trademark owner. All trademarks and brands inside this book are for clarifying purposes only and are owned by the owners themselves, not affiliated with this document.

CopyScape Verified April 27, 2015
Edited May 20, 2015

Contents

Chapter 1: Leadership Principles

Often people confuse leadership with a certain position. We would want to get to the top of the corporate field and hold positions such as CEO, MD, COO or other positions such as President, Principal, General or any other. We see these positions as leadership. People assume until they get a position of this type, they are not a leader. This is a wrong mindset. Leadership is not a position but behavior. How we react in every situation determines if we are leaders or not. Leadership is taking responsibility and making decisions at all times regardless of the position we are in. Most people who have risen to the top positions didn't just find themselves there. It's through effort and exhibiting leadership qualities at whatever situation and position they were in and hence could be trusted with even more demanding positions. If you want to be a leader, start now and take responsibility in whatever area you are in, bring about positive change and then you can get to any position you want. Your behavior, actions and attitude will improve your leadership credentials. With these, people will notice and will trust you with even greater responsibilities.

Leading by influence

Leaders bring out the best from their team. There are many ways to do this, you can coerce, threaten, intimidate or lead by example. Leading by example is the best way to get the best form your team. People are generally rebellious and will loathe anyone who commands them around. But when they are shown the way and see their leader doing exactly what he expects from them, then they strive to do their best. Set the best example that you'd like the people you lead to follow. Practice what you preach and soon you'll find that you won't even have to tell people what they need to do, they'll just be observing you and doing what it is you are doing.

You can influence people positively or negatively by your actions. You must make sure that all your actions and words are interpreted to mean what you would like to achieve. Otherwise, you lose your credibility as a leader.

Leaders make an impact

We all know of great leaders in history from different fields. These are people we have never met but get to hear of a lot. This is because of the impact they made. I'll give you an example that we can relate with easily. I presume we all know Steve Jobs. Yeah, this is a good example of a leader who left his mark. In fact I'll be relating some of the leadership qualities with him in this book. He brought about the technological evolution we have all enjoyed. He was a great leader in the entrepreneurship field who shall be remembered by many generations. This is the kind of impact that should be aimed for. What shall people remember of you as a leader? As much as leaders want to make people achieve a desired goal, the overriding motivation of any leader in whatever field they are in would be to leave an impact on society.

Leaders are visionary

One characteristic present in all leaders is that they have a vision and want to achieve it. Without a vision, you cannot lead others. Where will you be taking them? A good leader has a clear vision, communicates this vision to those that he leads, determines what action each team member will undertake to contribute to the achievement of the vision and finally coordinate all these actions. So the starting point is the vision. Some leaders have a clear vision they want to implement but fail to communicate it clearly to their team. They just point out what needs to be done. They only communicate what everyone has to do. This is not effective in the long run since without a clear understanding of what the team needs to achieve, there are bound to be misunderstandings. Each person you lead should be inspired by your vision to the extent that they are proud to contribute their efforts to achieve it.

Leaders are flexible

As a leader, you should strive to be as flexible as you can. Flexibility enhances decision making, enhances teamwork and problem solving when a dispute arises.

We have all been in situations where a small problem that could have been solved by an intervention from the leaders escalates due to inflexibility. Remember you are leading people, and as such, situations arise where not everything goes as we had hoped or planned for. We need to be flexible enough to make quick decision to situation that arise. Let me give a personal example here, I used to work under a manager at a financial institution who was extremely flexible. Our team loved him since when a problem arose; he could quickly analyze it, understand what caused it and provide a solution. This led to high levels of efficiency across the team. However, flexibility doesn't mean we change our core values; rather it applies in behaviors and attitudes. For instance, we can't be flexible to accommodate mediocrity from a team member.

Effective Leaders are humble

As a leader, you should always be humble. Being humble doesn't mean being a pushover or someone who people can ignore; rather it means having the ability to accept your weaknesses and acknowledging when you are wrong. If you manage this as a leader, you gain a lot more respect from your followers. If one of your followers or team members is better that you in a certain area, acknowledge it and give them room to do what they are good at without feeling threatened. Too many leaders are always looking over their shoulder and would even go to the extent of suppressing the strengths of one of their followers because they feel like they can take their position. This is a sign of insecurity and weakness. Humble leaders are well liked and inspire people since it's viewed as a sign of strength.

As a leader, you should show respect at all times to all people. It doesn't matter whom you are dealing with, be very respectful. People don't have to do anything for you as a leader to earn your respect. Respect even those people who get on your nerves.

Time management

Time is one of the most critical resources that a leader will be tasked to manage. How you manage your time and that of your organization will determine if you are a good leader or not. Time is constant and once wasted can never be recovered. We always find ourselves with more demands on our limited time. However, since we can't create more time, we need to manage our demands and deal with them in a smart way. As a leader you'll have a ton of email to read and respond too, numerous meetings, voicemails, and a desk full of work and so forth. This is on top of the team you need to direct, inspire and guide to achieving their goals. You also want time to improve yourself as a person. All these things can stress you out due to the limited time you seem to have.

An effective leader will have a strategy of proper time management for their organization. This is achieved by setting goals, priorities and action plans. Goals help us achieve our targets by detailing what we need to do every day. Goals should be SMART-Specific, Measurable, Achievable, Realistic and Time bound. The fact that every action will be bound by a time frame; it will help us in our time management better since we are able to review progress. For a leader, this is critical since you are managing your own time and that of others under you.

Another way to manage time effectively is having priorities. The leader and his/her team should identify and list priorities so that at any one time, everyone knows what needs to be done at any particular time. A calendar of activities detailing every task that should be done and when it should be done saves on time. Deadlines are observed when people are better prepared psychologically to expect certain tasks at certain times.

Chapter 2: Leading by Example

Great leaders lead others by their example. They do exactly what they say and this inspires their followers to do what they are told. Have you ever been in a workplace where the boss asks everyone to report early and leave late whereas they are never on time and leave any time they wish? What happens over time, people will lose trust in them and will not care much of what they say in the future. This is because in their eyes, they are not a credible leader. Even when that kind of boss wants to pass on some important communication, people might tend to take it casually. The opposite is true for a leader who gets to work before everybody else and leaves after everyone else has left. They will not even need to ask others to come in early. They will be inspired to do so by the example he sets.

Leadership is all about showing people what they need to do and guiding their efforts through good example. How you present yourself to your team speaks a lot. People will feel motivated to follow someone who influences by actions rather than by words. There are a few action points that I want to take you through to set a good example to your team.

Set a standard of excellence

As a leader, you expect your team to be excellent in their work, the question is, have you set the bar for this excellence? Being a leader comes with great responsibility as you should be the standard of excellence for your team. They should look at you and strive to achieve such a level. Set this bar as high as possible and live to it. Remember to be an effective leader; people must model their actions to yours. All your actions and behaviors should showcase excellence. Not any one time should people question your actions in regards to excellence because once they do this, then your credibility as a leader will be on the line. Human beings have this knack of getting awed and even almost worshiping someone who has risen above mediocrity. Strive to be that person as a leader. Excellence should be a norm to you to maintain the confidence and authority over your team.

Deliver results

Just like any other member of the team, a leader may have their work cut out for them. In most instances, you'll have the most challenging of tasks. These tasks will always influence the tasks of the other members of your team. In whatever it is you do, make sure you deliver results. A leader who can't deliver doesn't deserve to lead others. In any case, how will you question other people's results if you can't produce results yourself? You may have worked very hard to be where you are today but it's not the time to relax and watch others work; it's time for you to work harder if you are to achieve your vision. Past results won't matter to your current team; they want to see what you can do now. Don't give them an opportunity to question if you should be a leader. If you set targets with them, have just as high of a target for yourself and make sure you exceed it. When the leader performs the whole team performs. Never give an excuse as a leader regarding your performance.

Value the people you lead

One important thing that you need to keep in mind is that you lead people. Thus, you need people management skills, good communication skills and you need to nurture relationships. People work optimally when they feel valued and respected. When a leader is honest, fair and open, people will respect them and work their best with them. There will be no resentment which is very common in many employees. If you walk around asking people if they like their bosses, you'll find that many people won't have any kind words to say of them. However, if you look at the successful organizations, you realize that people respect their leaders since they feel valued. Make everyone feel important no matter what they are doing, since they all add up to what makes the organization.

Promote teamwork

In modern times, people work in teams. As you have noticed in this book, I am talking about leading a team not individuals. When people work as a team, they are more effective than when they work as individuals. The team can be two people or even a whole organization. As a leader, you will be responsible for creating the team(s) and making sure they function as intended. You will need to set the example to encouraging. Work with and listen to your team and in turn, you will be showing them that you value teamwork. The leader is ultimately responsible for making individuals work effectively in teams and enjoy it. Teamwork results in a higher quality of work, less fatigue, trust among members and greater interpersonal relationships. The leader must feel and be felt as part of the team.

Resolving conflict

Leaders need to set an example of how conflicts should be resolved within the team. Be quick and fair in settling any dispute that may arise within the team. Resolving conflicts is the hallmark of a great leader. Never allow divisions within your team due to poor handling of conflicts. Ultimately, be fair and honest. Have a good understanding of the problem and communicate the solutions clearly. The best way to resolve conflicts is to have a good understanding of your team right from the beginning. When disagreements arise, you'll be in a good position to intervene. If a conflict is not resolved properly, then resentment will inevitably arise and productivity will take a hit.

Always act exactly the same way you would like your followers or team to act. Take the high road as a leader and let your team follow you. Remember they are looking up to you to guide them. There's no better way of guiding people than letting your actions speak. Take the example of an army general who fights alongside of his men versus the general who orders his soldiers to go fight while he stays behind in a secure place. The soldiers being led by a general on the frontline will feel motivated to fight and win the battle whereas the others will feel abandoned and unmotivated.

Chapter 3: Adaptability to Change

Being able to adapt to change is one character trait of today's successful leaders. In the business and political spheres, change is now occurring at very fast rates and any person especially leaders who are unable or unwilling to adapt to it, find themselves thrown into oblivion. This change brings about new opportunities, more effective ways of carrying out tasks and greater efficiency at the workplace. A leader must be well placed to accept change and use it to further his team's efficiency.

A 2008 study conducted by the Economist Intelligence Unit, entitled Growing Global Executive Talent, showed that the top three leadership qualities that will be important over the years ahead include: the ability to motivate staff (35 percent); the ability to work well across cultures (34 percent); and the ability to facilitate change (32 percent). The least important were technical expertise (11 percent) and "bringing in the numbers" (10 percent).

The world as we know it today has become more of a global village due to advances in technology. This makes the challenges faced by leaders today to be unique. Businesses are competing on a global platform serving people with diverse needs. This requires leaders to be flexible enough to change according to these needs. Just like in evolution, the strongest leaders today are not those who are bright but those who can adapt to change. So if you are a leader or want to be a leader, you need to keep up with the change.

There are various ways leaders position themselves to be highly adaptable to change. It's a combination of behavior, mindset and values. Let's look at the factors that enable us to get ready for change.

Innovation

Innovation is one way which keeps us from going to oblivion. Constantly remaining innovative should be one of your key qualities as a leader. When we talk of innovation, it does not only come in the products or services we offer but also in all our processes. The leader should be on the lookout for new ways of doing things. The team will help and it's the duty of the leader to remain open minded and critically analyzes any suggestions put forward. Let's take an example of one of the most profitable company in the world which is also one of the most valuable brands, I am talking about Apple. When Steve jobs was taking over the company it was in debt and almost collapsing. What he did was to find new ways of doing things. He shared his vision with his team and together they embarked on the path of innovation. They revolutionized the whole technology scene with new and superior products. That was not all; they came up with a new way of serving their customers. They concentrated on improving the quality of their service such that the minute a customer walked into an apple shop, they felt valued. This innovation drove them from a company facing collapse to the biggest brand in the world.

In the modern world, innovation is one of the surest ways to remain relevant. The leader is responsible for driving innovation by allowing the team to share ideas freely and directing their efforts to what is important.

Low levels of anxiety

People able to adapt to change have low levels of anxiety. The human nature wants us to remain to what we are used to. We are most comfortable doing things we have been doing as this brings about a sense of security. However, if we remain doing these things, we might be left behind in our fast paced world. Thus as a leader you shouldn't be anxious of change. Even your team should be highly adaptive to change. Anxiety is the number one reason that holds people back from implementing something new. Most anxiety is driven by negative emotions, past unpleasant experiences, or even fear of the unknown.

Being a leader, you must work around any anxiety you have as well as that of your team members by carefully analyzing all situations and taking calculated risks. Create an environment for your team where every member feels free to bring forth new ideas, share experiences and fears. No member should feel threatened or intimidated in the course of their duty. Maintain enthusiasm amongst your team to avert any anxiety that may arise and remain optimistic.

Action

Being able to adapt to change requires a leader to be action oriented. You shouldn't just be prepared for change but also ready to take appropriate action when necessary. Being the leader, don't just direct others to take the action you wish taken but also participate in it to increase the motivation. Great leaders are passionate about what action needs to be taken and will find themselves taking part in it and monitoring progress real time.

Confidence

Embracing change requires confidence. It's getting into the unknown without fear or anxiety. That's what confidence is all about. However, to identify and take advantage of new opportunities, we need to be ready to change. We can increase our confidence levels by having adequate preparation in place. A great leader should be able to prepare their team to explore new territory and take risks and be confident while doing so.

Change in leadership style

Different leaders use different leadership styles. However, even this needs not be rigid. A great leader should have different leadership skills to apply in different situations. This enables you develop solutions quickly enough. When you learn where and when to use each of these styles, you achieve your goals and vision.

As an adaptable leader you should

- Be open to new ideas.

- Adapt to very situation.

- Handle emergencies and unexpected demands

- Solve problems creatively

- Learn new tasks, procedures and technologies and apply them

- Have interpersonal adaptability, know how to deal with people from diverse backgrounds

- Be able to change or adapt your strategy to suit circumstance

Chapter 4: Great Leaders are Great communicators

One of the common qualities among great leaders is their ability to communicate effectively. As a leader, you are guiding people to achieve certain goals and you need to make sure they not only understand your vision but also know what needs to be done at each stage. Being a great communicator doesn't mean being a great talker. You can talk well but achieve little communication. Some leaders are great talkers but not good communicators. This is partly due to what we are taught at school. Grammar, pronunciation and syntax are overemphasized from an early age at the expense of clearly outlining your thoughts so that those listening understand exactly what you want them to get.

Talking is only half of good communication, the other half is active listening. In order to be a great communicator, you have to be a great listener. As a leader, you'll be responsible for communicating not only to your team, but also to all elements that interact with your organization. They may be customers, investors, other organizations, regulators and any other. You should be able to know how to communicate with each of these groups of people effectively. It may require you to employ different communication and leadership styles. For instance the style you use when delivering some information to your employees should not be the same you use on your customers. Be ready to adapt your style to suit your audience.

Communication comes in two ways, verbal and nonverbal. Verbal is the most obvious but a lot of communication happens through no verbal means as well. Leaders need to learn how to decode nonverbal communication. You also need to learn how to pass on information to your team through nonverbal means. Some nonverbal cues include posture, eye movement, facial expressions and use of hands. Listen actively to both the verbal and nonverbal means to get the full reaction. Some common barriers to effective communication are assumption that the message is received and understood, use of a wrong medium, lack of emotions when delivering the message, communication by intimidation, and use of the wrong communication style.

How to be a Leader

Being a leader, you'll be spending much of your time interacting with others. If there's one thing you'll need to have in order to be effective as a leader, it is good communication skills. Have you ever been in a meeting and everybody seemed so bored and sleepy and barely listening? Only their bodies are present but their minds are far off. Don't be this kind of a leader. When you talk to those whom you lead, you should stimulate their emotions and aspirations. When you involve emotions, people will listen and apply what you tell them. Never bark orders to your followers. This will be the fastest way to being a bad communicator. People will pretend to listen for fear of your authority but in the real sense they don't understand what you mean. When this happens, it becomes extremely difficult to achieve anything within your team. Remember, communication is a two way streak; you also need to listen as well to feedback which informs you how well your communication has been understood.

People look up to their leaders for inspiration. Thus, in all your communication, you should offer inspiration and motivation, to the extent that people look forward to hearing you and talking to you. Your mode of communication will also be very vital for avoiding conflicts. Most problems facing organizations are as a result of poor communication. Poor delivery of information and poor feedback ultimately reflects in the performance of any entity. In today's world, interpersonal skills are one of the most sought after in most organizations when it comes to selecting leaders. The bottom line of this is that leaders lead people and to lead people, you need to have great interpersonal skills. One way to achieve this is to be a great communicator. Being a great communicator is the result of carefully choosing your words, choosing to be a great listener and connecting emotionally with people. You have to be open-minded and learn how to interact with people of different backgrounds. In the next chapter, we shall be looking at dealing with difficult people and situations. You should learn how to get your message through and obtain feedback even when you deal with these difficult people. Thus it's not surprising that great leaders get along with all kinds of people and get information across efficiently. They do this by having a good sense of situational and contextual awareness. They read people emotions, attitudes, moods, concerns and values and align them to their communication. Always align your message to the needs of your individual team members.

As a leader, aim to have personal communications rather than having corporate communications. Bring down all barriers that inhibit this personal communication between you and your team. Never let any one of your followers think twice about approaching you for any kind of conversation, be it work related or otherwise. When you create this environment, people trust you and will be open to converse with you. With this you get to put across information more clearly and get instant feedback. The more personal conversations you get with your team, the more efficient your communication becomes. There's this saying, 'people don't care how much you know until they know how much you care'. Leaders in the business sphere used to rarely interact with their colleagues and thus remained strangers. When an important communication needed to be passed down, they would do in highly structured means. This is not effective communication as you don't even know whether people have understood what you want from them and it might take a lot of time for you to tell. In today's, world, there's no luxury of time, you need people to understand what you mean as fast as possible and get their feedback almost immediately. To do this you need to be simple and concise. Be specific and emphasize on the main points.

Good leaders know when it's time to shut up and listen. Often, average leaders will only entertain one way communication without offering any chance for feedback or dissenting opinion. But that's not what you want to be, you want to be able to listen to all views, even those that are opposing your stand. When you listen to these views, do so with an open mind, not with the intention to argue or convince. In most cases, opposing and criticizing views make us better at what we do since they introduce a new perspective that we might not have thought about. Have deep and open conversations with every person you lead with the intention of understanding what they think and what needs to be done. When you do, you are on your way to being a great leader.

To get a message across, you need to know what are talking about. Being a leader, you have to intimately understand what you want your organization to get from you, otherwise, they won't take you seriously. If you don't have expertise in the subject matter, you would need to find someone who does to deliver the message. We are in an age of information where people will quickly tell whether you know what you talking about or are just faking it. Don't force it, you either know it or you don't. Unfortunately many leaders fail in this since they feel that they need to address their people and only end up misinforming rather than communicating.

Good communication skills need to be cultivated by all people and particularly leaders. When we communicate effectively, we get half the job done. Leadership is all about communication.

Chapter 5: Dealing with Difficult People and Situations

In the world we live in, there are kinds of people. Being a leader means sometimes you'll have to lead people who may be defined as difficult. It will be your responsibility to make sure that goals are achieved nonetheless. Who are difficult people? This is a question that isn't straight forward. Many people will tend to quickly think of the hostile and aggressive personalities as the difficult people. In fact many people won't classify themselves as difficult and would even take it as an insult if you told them they are. We look at some people as being difficult. Let me say that being difficult isn't necessarily a bad thing; it's about personality traits that are hard wired in us.

There are seven categories of difficult people according to Robert M Branson in his book "Coping with Difficult People" written in 1981.

- Hostile-aggressive
- Complainers
- Silent and unresponsive
- Super agreeable
- Know-it-all experts
- Negativists
- Indecisive

I know you have started nodding your head as you might have worked with such kinds of people. All these character traits are unique and people might not even realize they are difficult. For instance, the super agreeable people are difficult since they always agree with you as a leader even when you might be wrong. They don't offer ideas and always say yes. This is a pretty frustrating and difficult group of people you need to deal with.

Being a leader, you need to understand each person and their character trait. Have an open mind and realize they are not being deliberately difficult. Their intentions are good and attitude is proper. Social and economic backgrounds might have informed us who they are. People who have grown up in an environment where they barely got by with life will tend to have security issues and won't take risks even when they are past that phase of their life. What such kinds of people will need from their leader is constant encouragement and motivation. It's constructive to note that if you ever question the intention and attitude of those you lead, then that person is not difficult. That is a destructive and malicious person. You have no business leading such a person.

Since difficult people are not going to disappear, you need to learn to deal with them right from the onset provided they are not having a detrimental effect on your organization, don't do away with them. There are people who are generally aggressive and will rub many shoulders the wrong way. However they get work done. They are highly energetic and probably what they lack is interpersonal skills. You can't do away with such kind of a productive employees; you'll need to manage them which is one of your duties as a leader. Other types of difficult people are the chronic complainers. They will complain about anything and everything. They spend more time looking at the problem than looking at the solution. These people mean well but you need to refocus their energies to look for solutions rather than complain. They mostly are very capable of coming up with solutions but will first feel the need to complain.

Here are some tips on how to deal with difficult people

Establish facts

When you encounter a situation, aim first to establish all the facts before you offer a solution. Fast actions are needed from all leaders in today's world, but first establish the facts. Don't allow emotions get in the way of your decision making. You might tend to get angry with a person since they didn't react the way you envisioned, but this shouldn't lead you to making an emotionally charged decision. You might only regret it later. Don't yell or get overly animated. Remember people are looking up to you as a leader for guidance. You might be getting worked up on the inside but you must master your self-control. Remember we said communication can be through nonverbal means as well, so master your body's language and don't let it give away your emotions. If you allow emotions to get in the way, your team will see you as not being objective. When dealing with difficult people, this would be the last thing you want.

Don't be personal

It's very tempting to get things personal when you encounter a difficult person. As a leader, don't get this low, maintain professionalism and instill sense in this person. Most probably, you'll be solving a conflict brought about by this kind of an employee don't let any personal misgivings to come in the way of your judgment. Establish facts of this issue at hand and offer direction.

Have courage

You need to be fearless when dealing with different character traits. You might be a leader and one of you employees proves to be aggressive and disruptive to the other team members. You need to be able to tell and show them how their behavior or mode of operation is limiting the others. You might not want to slow them down, but refocusing their energies to a different operational strategy might work best for everybody.

Respond decisively

When you deal with difficult people or situations, you need to act decisively. Never bring about doubts as regards your leadership abilities. Be confident and speak with conviction. Work to avert a crisis by dealing with issues as soon as they arise.

Leader from all walks of life encounter difficult people and difficult situations all the time. It's how you deal with them and turn them around to your advantage that determines if you are really a great leader. And still on this, you should look inside to know if you are a difficult person as well. You might be the cause of the problems you are trying to solve in the first place.

Chapter 6: Good Leaders are Motivational

Motivation is what drives us to work. However, people are no always motivated due to a variety of reasons. Many employees will just go to work to earn their monthly or biweekly paycheck. They won't care what they do provided they produce just the bare minimum to get the pay. Your work as a leader is to provide the motivation required to turn such kind of people to devotees who look forward to work since they are working towards achieving a defined goal.

One way of improving motivation is to value the input of your staff. People will improve their attitude once they realize that their opinions are being valued. This raises their self-esteem and they will look forward to work. The opposite is true. If as a leader you are always dismissing your employee's opinions, then soon enough, you'll have an unmotivated team. Give your team the freedom to use their ideas. When people are part of a successful team, and feel to have contributed to the success, they feel motivated. This is more that what a financial incentives would achieve. The thing with money is that we pretty much forget after we receive it. On the other hand if our efforts are recognized and appreciated, we feel valued and have that extra boost to work harder. You need to make your staff feel as an integral part of the organization. They should relate to it and own it. Strong leaders are the number one motivation to any workforce far out ranking financial incentives.

Energize your team. How do you do it? By Leading by example, communicating clearly, and challenging everyone. You can't motivate people whereas you are doing what is not right. Start by outlining your vision, goal and action plan. These should be aligned with your team's vision and aspirations. Then everything you do and say must be consistent with the vision. For instance if you value teamwork and encourage it within your tam, you should be at the forefront in helping out others in their tasks. Don't wait to be asked for help, if you notice any member struggling offer to help and others will take this cue.

Challenging is also a way to motivate. People are always in need of a challenge, provided it's within their abilities and is attainable. They will work hard to achieve it. Great leaders challenge their followers often. Make the challenge as interesting and creative as possible. Stimulate the mind of your employees and let them have the freedom to implement. However, after they achieve the set goals, be the first to congratulate them.

Encouragement is another way through which leaders motivate. As a leader, your role is to harness other people's skills and talents and direct them towards achieving a common goal. You realize your role is not to dictate what needs to be done but letting others do what they have to do. Your role is just to direct the efforts of different people to a shared vision. Empower others to use their minds creatively in achieving intended results. Provide all they need to do this. You might provide coaching to refine skills. Recognition of little efforts is another way to encourage performance.

Another way to motivate your team is getting to know them more personally. How is one doing in their social lives? What are some important events they have in their life? Work is just a single component of life. It's not the most important and a great leader realizes that people need to advance their social and spiritual lives. Without these, they may become unbalanced people only focused on work which will lead to burnout. Form a strong relationship with your team such that you know what's happening in everybody's life at any particle moment. We have all heard of many cases where people who worked side by side with each other, interacting daily, but never had the slightest idea of each other's life outside work. Encourage your team to live positively, have healthy relationships and have more balanced life. I used to have a boss who wouldn't stand seeing anybody in the office after 5.00 pm. He always wanted us to have time for other equally important aspects of our lives. This translated to more energy and extra motivation at work.

Chapter 7: Traits of an Effective Leader

Competency alone doesn't make a leader. To be an effective leader you have to have a combination of qualities. Let's look at these qualities.

Passionate

Every great leader is passionate about their role. Passion is what fuels us. It provides the energy to keep going. Without passion, you'll end up just being nothing. Donald Trump said, "Without passion, you don't have energy; without energy, you have nothing." Passion enables us to have a clear vision of what we want to achieve. Great leaders see the results way ahead. Even when they are directing the efforts of their team, they have a clear understanding on the end result. They passionately sell this vision to the team. The passion will soon rub off and every member of the team will feel a need to work towards achieving the vision.

Passion doesn't go unnoticed, people will notice how much effort you put in your job, how different you are and how determined you are to provide a solution. This will be reflected in your teams' attitude, your service/product and in everything you offer. If you are an employee in a company, your superiors will notice all the motivation and zeal you put in your job and sooner than you think, promotion will be coming your way. You'll have shown that you can be trusted with more responsibilities and deliver.

Awareness

A leader needs to have a high sense of awareness. This should be contextual and situational awareness. This awareness will help with every action you take, every word you speak and the image you portray to those who lead. The great leader Mahatma Gandhi was a model in this. He advocated for nonviolent resistance to colonial rule. He encouraged his followers to seek out ways to agitate for their independence without ever being violent. This is a person who people looked up too for inspiration and in all his actions he portrayed the image of nonviolence no matter the circumstance. As a leader, always have a high sense of awareness and realize all your actions should be consistent with what people expect from you.

Focus

As a leader you should be extremely focused. Plan ahead and organize your diary well in advance. Always envision how a situation may turn out and have alternatives in place. Remember people look up to you to provide solutions and if you can't, you'll lose credibility as a leader. Your decisions will have intended impacts and also some impacts you didn't plan for, plan ahead for this by having different strategies. Establish processes and routines aimed at delivering success. Monitor these regularly and be flexible enough to change any which limits your team's potential.

Decisiveness

As a leader you will have to make decisions on a daily basis. Some of these decisions will be tough to make but will need to be made. Decisiveness is the ability to make the right decision at the required time. The decisions made must not be the most convenient at the time but the most appropriate. It might inconvenience some people but the greater good has to prevail. To be decisive, you will need to be firm, ooze authority and respected across the board. People should have faith that you took the decision in the interests of everybody and no ulterior motives were at play.

Accountability

As a leader you are ultimately responsible for the performance of your team. Never fail to take responsibility and resort to blame games. You are responsible for any failure by individual members of the team since you were in charge and could have noticed weaknesses and taken remedial steps early on. When things go well don't bask in the glory alone, share the success with your team.

Leaders will need most of these traits to be successful in their work. They are fundamental regardless of the area of leadership you are in. leaders will also need to have some political shrewdness in them. Making decision where people are involved isn't easy and politic will definitely come in play. A leader should know how to balance out between opposing interests.

Conclusion

Leadership is a learned skill. The more effort we put in, the better we will become. Personal traits will play a major role in determining whether you'll be a successful leader but to a large extent, it's more of the conscious effort we put in. Cultivate your leadership traits all the time no matter the situation you are currently in. Life offers us a lot of opportunities to showcase our leadership abilities and it's upon you to seize them. Don't wait till you get to a certain position, this will never happen if you don't take the small opportunities that arise. In any case, leadership is not a position but an opportunity to influence. Work on any trait you feel you lack to make you an effective leader. If for instance you lack interpersonal skills, don't give up on your leadership dreams; actively develop this trait by learning how you should relate to people and applying it in real life.

Thank you again for purchasing this book! I Hope this book was of value to you. If so, please take the time to review it on Amazon. It would be greatly appreciated.

If this book was of value to you, you may also be interested in other books by Max Smart.

Consider looking up the book below:

How to Remember: Easy Steps to Retain and Remember

All books by Max Smart are available on Amazon so go ahead and read some more.